Lonely Women
Make Good Lovers

Lonely Women Make Good Lovers

Keetje Kuipers

AMERICAN POETS CONTINUUM SERIES NO. 212

BOA EDITIONS, LTD. ≈ ROCHESTER, NY ≈ 2025

Copyright © 2025 by Keetje Kuipers

All rights reserved
Manufactured in the United States of America

First Edition
23 24 25 26 7 6 5 4 3 2 1

For information about permission to reuse any material from this book, please contact The Permissions Company at www.permissionscompany.com or e-mail permdude@gmail.com.

Publications by BOA Editions, Ltd.—a not-for-profit corporation under section 501 (c) (3) of the United States Internal Revenue Code—are made possible with funds from a variety of sources, including public funds from the Literature Program of the National Endowment for the Arts; the New York State Council on the Arts, a state agency; and the County of Monroe, NY. Private funding sources include the Max and Marian Farash Charitable Foundation; the Mary S. Mulligan Charitable Trust; the Rochester Area Community Foundation; the Ames-Amzalak Memorial Trust in memory of Henry Ames, Semon Amzalak, and Dan Amzalak; the LGBT Fund of Greater Rochester; and contributions from many individuals nationwide. See Colophon on page 90 for special individual acknowledgments.

Cover Art: ") (XI" by Vivian Greven
Cover Design: Sandy Knight
Interior Design and Composition: Isabella Madeira
BOA Logo: Mirko

BOA Editions books are available electronically through BookShare, an online distributor offering Large-Print, Braille, Multimedia Audio Book, and Dyslexic formats, as well as through e-readers that feature text to speech capabilities.

Cataloging-in-Publication Data is available from the Library of Congress.

BOA Editions, Ltd.
250 North Goodman Street, Suite 306
Rochester, NY 14607
www.boaeditions.org
A. Poulin, Jr., Founder (1938-1996)

For Sarah

Contents

With Garbo in Palm Springs	11
At Forty, the Mountains Are More Green	13
Lonely women make good lovers,	14
Getting Back Together	16
The Magician at the Woodpile	17
Bleeding	18
At My Daughter's Riding Lesson	20
Spa Days	22
In the Outdoor Shower with My Pregnant Wife	23
I Didn't Know What I Didn't Know	25
Cremello Horse	26
I wasn't trying to steal her boyfriend,	27
Sehnsucht	28
Poikilothermic	29
Love Letter to a Friend I Cannot Reach	30
I, too, took pictures of my body	32
Brace Cove	33
Emesis	34
I Let Her Let Them	35
The day after your mom dies, I go to see the witches,	36
The Wound	37
Boat Puller / Bird Woman / Madame Charbonneau	38
Walking Lessons	42
Pregnant Girl Creek	43

Washing My Daughter's Clothes	45
Selfishness	46
My Mother Bought Me a Scarf	47
Interview	48
Crossing	49
Live Webcam: Ponte delle Guglie, Venice; March 2020	50
Multi-Generational Household	51
Eating Sea Urchin	52
At Our Hotel Under the Volcano	53
Playtime	55
Meat	57
Summer, Again	58
Season Finale	60
3,000 Miles Away from Home	62
Diapause	63
Eating an Orange Before Getting Out of the Swimming Pool	64
Googling My Ex	65
Greek Chorus	66
The Rats	70
Polished Rough	72
Now that we've been married all these years,	73

≈

Notes	75
Acknowledgments	77
About the Author	81
Colophon	90

If self is a location, so is love:
Bearings taken, markings, cardinal points,
Options, obstinancies, dug heels and distance,
Here and there and now and then, a stance.

—Seamus Heaney, "The Aerodrome"

With Garbo in Palm Springs

We're at the resort, the one with the forty-one
pools, and it's night so if we were up in the swaying
fronds of a palm tree, the ground would stretch before us
a green freckled thigh against a dark sheet. But Greta
and I are inside, perched on the edge of the bed,
watching my wife sleep. She's beautiful, we agree,
and my daughter, too, their blond hair spread against
the pillow like a silk scarf in a silent movie.
Though now Greta's impatient with all the watching,
the kid especially, so we go outside to smoke
her cigarettes, to lean our backs against the white
adobe walls and kiss for as long as it takes.
The electronic lock clicks behind us, a set
of perfect teeth, and I'm chasing Greta across
the lawn with its lemon trees I can smell in the dark,
past the lounge chair where someone's abandoned
the sort of wide-brimmed hat meant to keep us young,
over the patio still warm as skin from the sun's
relentless shining, toward the place where she's already
slipped off her dress and climbed into the water,
sidestroking with one arm and holding her smoke
aloft with the other. And if I say it's a dream,
it will have no power. And if I say it's real,
no one will ever believe me. But can't it
be both? I want to rub my body against her
perfect one. So I do. All my nubbly parts sanded
down against the smooth monument of her form,
ageless as the desert once was before we came here
and turned it into a golf course. Now only

my hunger—its vast, unquenchable fury—
interrupts the glow of each long leg as she traces
eggbeater circles in the blue depths beneath her.

At Forty, the Mountains Are More Green

Here the melting, there the glacier
already gone. All these years, I've watched
my body as if from a distance

nearly geologic: the comings and goings
of a thousand tiny fossils against my flesh.
Last night, beside my sleeping wife's form

in the ageless glow of my phone,
I scrolled past the before and after
of butt implants, celebs who maybe did

or didn't, and the pregnant model
who last week had the silicone removed
from her breasts. *I'll still have boobs,*

she said, *they'll just be pure fat.* Upstream,
they're taking out the dam, diverting
the creek. This morning, I woke to the dull

scalpel of dozers. Soon they'll loose the fish
from the chute and finally the bodies
within that body will be free.

Lonely women make good lovers,

sings the man on the country station,

but that's not how I
remember loneliness: mostly
too drunk to feel anyone's pleasure,

and the next morning

that pitiful kinship
of distance. Except for the night he
couldn't finish it—not in

the meadow, not in his truck—

until finally we stumbled
through the blue light
of his shared living room

because at the least

he needed some place
to put my hunger to bed.
In the morning he thought to make

the misadventure right

while I looked out the window,
examining the scars on the glass—
bird shit, a feather, unbroken blue sky—

the same way I look down at my hands

now, everything so plain, even
my pain, which I'd thought
anyone could see.

Getting Back Together

We sat around unpacking boxes. I had a baby
on the way, and the new nursery was still full of past lives
carefully wrapped in paper and taped shut. My family

had come down to help, and you were somewhere
miles away, as you had been for years, the two of us
clumsily circling the future like a pair of kites getting

tangled up the same tree. But then Aunt Jean bent over
to root through the bubble wrap, her fingers twisting
in studded pleather straps, a muttered *What's this?*

before triumphantly pulling it out: our old strap-on,
the blue dildo we'd taken to bed a decade earlier, purchased
from some old queen, probably not actually old, probably

younger than we are now, who'd lounged behind
the counter of a Philadelphia sex shop with pink hair
and an understanding smile. And I won't say

that was the moment my heart tipped back toward you—
we both know it took much longer—only that I began
then to sense the ways I might still be changed.

The Magician at the Woodpile

The blue tarp is covered in little pools
of water that shimmer like sequins
everywhere a wrinkle has gathered. I pull
it off with a flourish and start digging through
the kindling and logs until I find the dicks,
all of them, hidden in the back of the pile.
The dicks I took in my mouth. The dicks
that didn't ask permission. The dicks I loved
and the dicks I never really knew. I remember
holding them in my hands—how soft the skin,
how various the shapes—and cooing to each one,
You're the most beautiful dick I've ever seen,
as if wonder were the only register my voice
could work in. Now I stack the wood the way
the dicks must have learned at camp,
with the kindling at the bottom and the big
logs on top. I add the dicks last, like a little pink
crown of thorns. Then I light the whole thing on fire.
I expect to see spiders come running out, rats
even. I expect to hear screams. But there's nothing.
Just a fire making me warm, even as the sun
goes down at my back, everything but my face
suddenly in darkness, like I'm performing
a magic trick, like the magic trick is me.

Bleeding

The world is trying to kill me
one news story, one sneeze,
one bad president at a time.
And maybe I don't care
anymore if I'm dead. That's what
I used to think when she put
her fingers inside me —
I don't care if I die —it felt
so good. She loved my body
when it stank, when I hadn't
showered or brushed my teeth,
she loved it in cheap hostels
or in apartments haunted
by a stranger's cigarette smoke,
beneath the pale, hushed sheets
of her childhood bedroom,
when I was ill, on drugs, the day
after I'd gotten out of the hospital,
and every week of every month
for years, nothing stopping us,
her hands turned bright red
with the blood of loving me.
We'd put a towel down to sop
up the mess, as if I'd died,
as if she'd killed me, our bodies
collapsed on top of each other,
just one more murder-suicide,
everything but the gun, the knife,
the man to complete the scene.
And here we still are, despite every

loaded weapon, pulling a red
scarf from between my legs,
and me mumbling *I could die, I could
die*, but still somehow alive.

At My Daughter's Riding Lesson

What was the name of that bar
where I kissed a blonde in a photobooth,

her husband just the other side
of the oilcloth curtain? Or the street

where our apartment sat above the train, soot
speckling the ceiling like a bad lung

we lived inside of? The letters we wrote then—
not *love*, but some bright threads birds

might down their dull nests with. Now rain
on the roof of the barn, swallows back

after their long winter away, memory no more
than a season. Sometimes I long

for the kind of sadness inside of which
no one could ever touch me. In the snowmelt

puddles beside the barn, we once found blood
pooled on the surface like oil, a thing held

deep inside, never meant to be brought up.
But I know what it would mean to choose

to return to the world after real loss—
to my heart with its broken tremolo, to this girl

on a horse, the reins in her still-soft
hands—because I do and I do and I do.

Spa Days

I drive through the yellow ribcage of maples
arching the road, past the butch woman I want
to be, raking leaves in her front yard, hair
slicked back at the sides. Yesterday, searching
the internet for winter tights, I found crotchless ones,
a model's diffident fingertips barely obscuring
the hairless glow of her pussy, and remembered
the years I spent lying on a table in a quiet room,
piped sound of harps descending from the ceiling,
while some other woman carefully made my body
as smooth and unthreatening as a child's.

I didn't hate those days, or the men I then took
to bed, though I was always trying to fuck my way
towards the woman I believed was hidden
inside each one of them. I knew it would require
a dive, a sinking past waves and midnight zones.
How strange to discover then what I've become
through that slow, fruitless searching—the water
itself, every dark, glitterless bit of it like the back
of a rhinestone: flat, matte surface where you
put the glue. And the music, all these years later,
still ringing in my ears from that distance above me.

In the Outdoor Shower with My Pregnant Wife

The old frisbee from Burger Chef, once red
but faded now the pale pink of my wife's
widening areolas, lies upturned
beneath the saltwater drip of our sagging
beach towels. This world is full of objects
succumbing to the gentle ebb of decay. But her body—
loosening breasts and blue-veined thighs caught
in a cascade of wet light as she turns
beneath the showerhead's senseless spray—
is not one of them. That low-blooming
shudder and heft at her hips can't compare
to her belly button's skin stretched taut
and thin, become the pale sail of a boat
screaming into harbor. I am here
to praise the way in which everything
I have ever loved about her body
is about to be ruined forever in the breaking
open. Tonight the wind will come up,
turn the towels on the line into fat bells,
churn the waves into a froth, drag the sand
out and leave it where our toes can't touch.
In the morning, the ocean will return
to its languid sheet, but the beach will be strewn
with the wreckage. I want already
the body scarred by stretch marks, the extra flap
of skin to hang soft at her waist, the feet
that will never again be quite so small.
I want to worship the body after the storm,
the one I'm imagining already
as she unfolds the straps from her shoulders

and peels the suit off, her skin covered in
those minute and glittering fragments of shell
some people insist on calling sand.

I Didn't Know What I Didn't Know

Rumor was she blew him after Geometry
out behind the baseball diamond, a kind of place

it confused me to learn existed. Not pretty—
homely is maybe what you would have called

my best friend. Her parents' house was filled
with leaves and the smell of vegetables. And I spent

more hours stretched across the rug of her attic room
than I did in my own bed. Did I ask her about him then,

our bodies parallel on the floor as we examined
the seam of her ceiling, her straw-like hair quivering

with the tic that twisted her face when nervous
or even happy, its flutter just at the edge of what

I could see without turning my head? I don't
remember. All I know is that she never told me.

I didn't understand shame then. My luck was a short
rope holding me always too close to myself.

Cremello Horse

I do not want to make your strangeness exciting.
It's too short a distance from wonder to terror,

and blue eyes in a horse is something wondrous.
Like you, I've been found strange. Like you,

I've glowed in a field at night and had nowhere
to hide: my high laugh, that birthmark, so many

things others could see but that I've had to twist
myself to examine. Once, in a circle of rapt faces,

a boy pushed my girl-body against a wall
with such force his touch could not have been far

from wonder. You've known it, too, horse—
the sugar cubes and wick of razor wire. *See*

how that feels? he said, as if I'd pushed him first.
And perhaps something in me had.

I wasn't trying to steal her boyfriend,

and he wasn't her boyfriend anyway. Just someone
beautiful she'd slept with once. I hadn't yet

learned the difference between a shadow cast
in the shape of my desire and the contract a body

makes with its own hunger. But I'd known beauty—
its currency, its power. So I wanted to sleep

with him, too. How I went about it wasn't
that remarkable. I simply made myself appear

to be a thing he'd want: not me, but something
I could easily be mistaken for, like a bird, say,

pretending to be another bird. What I
craved from him was harder to cage. *Beautiful,*

beautiful, I'd heard people praised all my life.
Not the bird at all—just the flutter that it raised.

Sehnsucht

Taking all my clothes off,
as my therapist reminds me,

is my specialty. Exposed, yes—
as these wild roses that grow

along the shore like crushed velvet,
a skirt washed up and dried

to salty rime—but that doesn't
mean seen. It doesn't mean

known. Getting naked fast
is what I do to collapse the distance

between myself and any
body that seems to want

to resist me. A falling away:
these shore birds who move

together, then shatter
like a mirror across the blue.

Poikilothermic

We take our chairs out into the sun where the small poodle can run laps round the bougainvillea or curl in the bowl made between the old lady's bathrobed knees. I sit across from her as she strokes its furred skull with her freckled hands. She is delighted to tell me how the scorpion—tiny, genius creature, glittering black bracelet splayed open against the yellow wall—kills itself. And I am delighted to listen. Though there was a time I wouldn't have wanted to learn anything about fear from another woman. As a child, she once saw a man catch a scorpion in a jar: he lit a match, put flame to a branch he then brought as close as he could to the glass. The girl inside the woman can remember seeing the scorpion's tail fly up to sting its own head—saving itself from a fire it could only feel as fear's shimmering heat. But as much as she remembers this, it isn't true. Beyond the stone wall, a marching band parades through the narrow street, firecrackers invisibly punctuating the air above her voice. I, too, have known untouchable fire and contracted in response. My second year in that city beside the sea, I did not want to die, and yet, from the outside, I must have looked like a woman with a dagger raised over her own blazing head.

Love Letter to a Friend I Cannot Reach

Sometimes, when I can't remember who I am,
I return to that café on the Place des Vosges
where years ago, in another life, you plunked lumps
of sugar into my espresso as if willing the cup
to overflow. But I was the one overfull, not caring
who saw me cry for my one true self—that self being imaginary,
lost somewhere in a future I could no longer see. Your
great uncle—who spoke no English, a Jew who had survived
and stayed, all his friends from the Résistance long dead—
fumbled the small square napkins like a useless deck
of tarot before pressing them to my wet face. Even remembering
now the cuffs of his tan trench coat as they gently bumped
against my cheeks, it is still difficult to remind myself
that the uncertainty of living in time is defined not by what we
cannot know of the world but what we cannot know
of ourselves. So am I ready to tell you your hair was a dark
cloud destroying itself on your shoulders? That I've loved you
always from the precise distance you've required?
That the pin I bought you of a head turned towards
its own twisted, wind-wrought tresses has become in my mind
these years later nothing less than your own visage, temples
now silvered to the metal's same dull shine, strands
of which I still long to tangle in my hands? Someone else
once explained to me that she loved me in spite of who I was.
I do not know her anymore, if I ever did. But you and I
sat there in those curved bamboo chairs all the Paris
bistros have, and I cried until my face was as bare
and charmless as your favorite bar in broad daylight,
no flickering candles or wine to soften its inherent need.
Why do I go back to such a moment? What comfort

can I find now that Uncle Willy, too, is dead, and I have not
seen your own sweet face in years? The separation
is unbearable. I am begging myself to taste the sugar, to keep
alive for you the one I thought I'd lost until we can meet again.

I, too, took pictures of my body

naked. Or let my best friend take them
for me. The little disposable cameras
I bought at the market, slim boxes
of cardboard and plastic light in my hand
as a dead bird. When we'd shot a whole
roll, I pedaled to the shop where the man
who on another day might hand my mother
an envelope of glossy family prints
waited behind the counter. Once, he called me
beautiful and asked if I was a model,
pushing the paper sleeve toward me
as if my body existing in the world
outside itself were something I already
understood rather than the thing
I was using those pictures to find out. I was
a girl, had never been touched
beneath my clothes. Though there I stood —
for anyone to see or even press a thumb to — first
wrapped tightly in a sheet, and in the next
with the cloth dropped at my feet, shadowed
strips of film forgotten on the floor.

Brace Cove

The famous painter rendered this cove two hundred

years ago in the empty transparencies of blues
and whites. Only one set of hands making

the brushstrokes, determining from that day on

how we might remember a place in time. If I think
too hard about the way you unbuttoned

my jeans that afternoon, your urgency to undo

the thing I'd said by forcing me to let you enter
my body one last time, I might walk down

to the water, past the sound of bees working

the husks of wild allium, and just keep going. It doesn't
matter where your hands are now. They finished

laying down their paint years ago.

Emesis

From her perch on the docent's gloved wrist,
she watched us with the eyes of any creature
handled too much: featherless head a closed
door, body a mask of silence. In the steep
twilight descending like the backwards
count of a nurse's voice leading a patient into
unconsciousness, the handler explained to
our circle the generalities of the species—the
turkey vulture's primary form of self-defense
is the regurgitation of semi-digested meat that
is then vomited onto a predator's face—and
the particularities of this one, who had come
to them with a broken wing. I have places
on my body knitted back together by unseen
hands, scars laid while I slept the sleep of
the unknowing: one above the belly button,
and another below where two fingers must
have parted the dark hair before shaving a
path. Does she remember the first faces to
peer toward her as she surfaced? Every time
I try to write what those hands did, instead
I plunge my own fingers inside to pull up
the voice of the surgeon in post-op: *I usually
have to pay women to take their clothes off for
me.* Oh, the shudder of her black-feathered
shoulders. Oh, the bile rising in her throat.

I Let Her Let Them

Because my daughter is afraid. Because she checks
and double-checks the doors, the windows, the ones
even that hang thirty feet above the ground. Because
there might be a person, a man, an invisible breeze,
something bad and she'd *never see mommy again* —

I let her catch as many crabs as she wants. She turns over
rock after rock, pries up their heavy, barnacled sides, scars
her palms and shins with their sharp-bladed prehistoric shells
as she flips them damp-belly-up and squeals, then scoops
the runners from the sand. I let her take the big ones,

the small ones, the tiny ones like bloodless ticks. I let her
let them run sideways up her arms and scuttle across
the backs of her hands. I let her chuck them into buckets
she sloshes when she walks, let her stare down into the depths
as they circle each other, poking and stampeding in their terror.

I let her pin them on their backs until they're dizzy and sick
with fear. I even let her take one home. Wan, spotted, unusually
pretty. She brings it into our house and leaves the pail
in the hallway she's scared to walk down at night. Where
she forgets about it until morning when it doesn't stir.

The day after your mom dies, I go to see the witches,

and their tall hats slip through the October crowds
like covens of wicked fish. But here in Salem, we know
all the real witches are dead and everywhere else
it turns out they're dying, too. Your mother
was a witch to me, the good kind, who loved
animals and children and the spring against
her skin. Her hair was the color of the moon
above the barn at night when she went to visit
with the horses she collected like scuffed pennies,
leaning her strong face against each bridge of bone.
I don't know much about gentleness, but I know
it was her magic, and like any mother, she employed it
imperfectly, sometimes casting too much of a spell
and other times not enough. When I set the blue asters
on Goody Martin's empty grave, I leave them
for your mom, who never meant to hurt a fly, and for you
and me and the gentle witches we want to be.

The Wound

Few know where the depths are or can
recognize them; or, if they do, are afraid.
—Theodore Roethke, *On Poetry and Craft*

It was the winter the dog swallowed

a sewing needle. A crew had been hired
to bring the cedar down limb by limb, the man

at the top like a trapeze artist in a melancholic's

circus. When I went to the garden where the poet
had drowned and asked the groundskeeper

to show me the place—the *exact* place—

he looked me in the eye and shook his head.
You, child, were learning the four phases of plant

regeneration, and wanted to explain to me the way

evergreens bud. *Kiss me,* I said. *Right here,*
and pointed to my temple. You always hated it

when I let you tell me something I already knew.

Boat Puller / Bird Woman / Madame Charbonneau

i.

My daughter comes home with the packet tucked
in her backpack. The pages we spread on

the kitchen table ask that she identify
Sacagawea's *spouse* and *personal*

hardships. Through the window's glass,
a Norway maple planted on the land

of the Salish turns purple with what I
understand to be spring's simmering rage. So

ii.

I try to see the woman more completely
the only way I know how: wet moment

my daughter ripped from my body
and into the world, the thrill of using

my tongue to move one language into
another, or every time I've done

what no one else would—and why?—for reasons
of my own beyond anyone else's

iii.

imagining, because I am complex
as any being—the bitterroot, the camas—

and, like her, can never be known. *Our
interpreter we find reconciles all*

*the Indians as to our friendly intentions,
a woman with a party of men is*

a token of peace. Her face a token
on the front of a coin. Minted: Philadelphia,

iv.

Denver, San Francisco, West Point. I have
held her shining in my hand—*although not*

*minted for circulation from 2012
onward because of general unpopularity*

with the public—the weight slight in my palm,
the understanding of its significance

depreciating by the day. The artist
had been told to be *sensitive to cultural*

v.

authenticity, and try to avoid creating
a representation of a classical European

face in Native American headdress.
When I asked my friend why she doesn't

smile in pictures, she said, *They want the stoic*
Indian, I give them the stoic Indian. The essence

Curtis thought he captured in his photographs
was nothing more than the privacy of individual

vi.

interiority. Still I try to grasp her
stubbornness. Sly wit and grief. The flicker

of pleasure. Anything but what they tell me
she was: compliant, helpful, mindlessly

brave. *Whatever the criticism aimed*
at his work, it is hard to ignore the beauty

of the images and the sensitivity, dignity
and respect with which he treated

vii.

the subjects in front of his lens. What made
her laugh? Which berry was a favorite

breaking on her tongue? What of her
satisfaction, or its truest predecessor,

desire? More than selflessness, more even
than survival. *If she has enough to eat*

and a few trinkets to wear I believe
she would be perfectly content

viii.

anywhere. She cannot be a picture
book, a coin, a good lesson for white

children. She cannot even be this poem's
dream of empathy. She was a girl.

She was a woman. How many people
have wanted something from her? I can't

call her to me by any name now,
in any language that I try so hard to speak.

Walking Lessons

I still don't know how we found ourselves there on the sidewalk,
your children drawing hearts and stars on the pavement
while slyly taking in my demonstration of grace, how to put
one foot in front of the other with smooth, careless-seeming
precision. I'd once been asked at an audition to display
a hidden talent, and mine had been walking, or gliding, really,
like a bird who instinctively knows to find the warm
currents of air that will push it upward, or one of those flying
squirrels whose entire body becomes an easy sail for capturing
the world's wind. That's what I was trying to show you—
how to move like it didn't hurt to perform the body you'd been
given. So in front of your house I walked a clean line, my arms
loose at my sides, my head up and back, oddly conscious
of the workings of my knees, but confident in that working.
Then I turned and looked back at you with a smile. *Walk*
ward me, I said. For critique. For a lesson. I won't describe
 body any more than that. And I won't describe yours either—
   endless ways it had so often gone unloved. It doesn't matter
    I thought I was doing that spring evening in the town
    n't seen you in for years, only that I hurt you
      to teach an act of artifice so encoded in my flesh
        realize I'd been practicing it all my life, putting one foot
        sly—so thoughtlessly—right in front of the other.

Pregnant Girl Creek

There's a girl leaned back against the chains
of the bridge, clutching her belly

through the thin rayon of her dress like it's
covering the underside of the sun

while her friend tells her to tilt her head
right or left for the photos

she's taking with a phone, each turn
making a stripe of pink

bangs flash across the girl's face like the fan
of a bird's fragile wing,

and what I mean is that she doesn't
have much money, and also

that I know her, which isn't possible since
the girl I know is dead,

her children born and half-grown already, nothing
of her own shimmering

left in this light-sieved moment but the memory
of her sweetness, which was true

as this creek is cold, even at the end when she'd lost
her kids and was ashamed

of herself, and I think about how careless people
like to say that it doesn't cost

anything to be kind, but that some of us know
the truth, which is that the price

of cracking yourself open to the world long enough
to feel love for a stranger,

which is the same as feeling love for yourself,
is dear, so that it hurts

more than a little to lean in as I pass by and spend it all
on this girl, telling her

how pretty those pictures are going to be.

Washing My Daughter's Clothes

Out the laundry room window, a swan
dips its head into lake water still
murky from last year's snow, surfaces

silt roping its neck. Some yellow flutter—
I don't know its name or even what
it's called—and then a turkey, so close

I almost miss the fat, dark shadow
of its awkward passing. My mother's
grandmother—uncomplaining, I've heard,

but sad—hanged herself in the one plumbed
back room of her house having made it
just as long as I have on this earth.

Something else I don't know much about.
She waited awhile, until her girls
were grown. She didn't leave a note. Women

in my family are like the bears I
haven't seen yet this season. You can't
predict their comings or their goings.

Selfishness

I used to sob in front of the dog—before he died,
before I had children or married my wife—his belly

helplessly pressed to the rug that smelled of his sweat
from years of waiting. I know he hated it, that it made

him uncomfortable, embarrassed even, if a dog
can feel the squeamishness of sympathy, like people I've

known who turned away from the sharp edges of my
breaking. Like them, he preferred me powerful, my hand

on his head or just beside the collar that told strangers
what I called him. Once at the city park he peed

on a stranger's leg—this creature who had always known
who to bark at and who to give his silence—leaning

into their body, gently, under a sky of weak clouds like
stuffing pulled from a couch. He must have known

something about them that I didn't. I cherished the idea
of his knowing, even as I cried, even if he didn't know.

My Mother Bought Me a Scarf

It came from a catalog. I opened
the plastic bag inside the plastic bag

and out tumbled fabric fine as flesh.
From the hem hung a thread I thought

to free with one swift tug. But this
was like pulling a river from the sea. Strand

of hair: long and black and woven all
its shimmering length. Of course

I wondered who she was. I read the tag
and closed my eyes until someone nearly

appeared to me. Let's not pretend I knew
her life. I wore the scarf most days.

As for the river, I didn't know what to do
with what I'd found, so I threw it away.

Interview

The elevator opened onto a corridor,
long and wood-paneled and lit
by the dim promise of windows.
I was walked down the hall, my cheap
flats soundless on the Oriental rug's
mute tongue. No voices, not even
the thoughtless song of breath
disturbed the air when we paused
at a room where four women bent
their scarved heads over a conference table,
hands like white latex birds descending
to piles of Swarovski crystals in silver
and gold. They dabbed glue onto the backs
of thick cell phones until each was covered
in faux jewels. The position was personal
assistant and the toughest question was:
What would you do if I saw a bouquet somewhere
but I couldn't remember the spot and I told you
I had to have it? Downtown they were still
clearing the rubble from the pit. I saw
the shop window, its gilt frame, the black
velvet drop cloth, orchids and lilies
lit by a single recessed bulb. I didn't
get that job, or the next one. I left the city
like so many others. But what wouldn't
we have given to find those flowers?
Nothing. Anything. Our lives.

Crossing

Waved to a halt by a woman in an oiled canvas
coat, we watched the first flurries of the season

from the truck's cab as they moved the yearlings
from the north pasture to the south. No one

wanted to be the first to go. Dark
hides veiled in a thin lace of flakes like the child-

sized bridal train for sale at the thrift shop
in town, they huddled at the gates making

the faint sounds of mercy. Behind them, men
and women on horseback moved through the scrim

of snow, impossible to know what they
called to each other as we watched their lips

from behind the glass. Today the world is
melt and muck, and from the high road I see

their bodies scattered — easy once again —
across the field. Yesterday is still

a land with a blanket pulled over its borders,
though each knows what it means to have crossed.

Live Webcam: Ponte delle Guglie, Venice; March 2020

Just two people, now three, and a dog at
the end of a leash. I keep waiting for
something to happen. A bomb. A bullet.
Two cross the bridge from opposite sides, dog
hanging back for a pee at the canal's
concrete edge. Ordinary. I may have
been there once, eating pastries, drinking cold
bitter sodas with my mother on wrought
iron chairs they put out so we could watch
the sun die each day. I could be there now.
In the grain of the camera's eye, their masks
could be imagined, which is what I'm trying
to do: imagine. I want to see how
close they will get to each other, how close

I can get to them. I come back later,
surprised it's night, one old lady pulling
a small cart of groceries. From the corner
of my screen, an empty water taxi
crosses the place where lamplight makes a school
of steel minnows against the surface. I
am trying to be present here. I
am trying to remember she is real,
the woman in the red shirt who just now—
this exact second, I tell myself—walks
back into the shadow of the alley
and disappears from my brief sight. Have I
never cared for anyone but myself?
And look what it took for me to know that.

50

Multi-Generational Household

In the middle of the night, I come downstairs
for a glass of water and find my father
in the kitchen, high as a kite, the dregs
from his vape pen making a murky cloud
around his head as he stuffs his mouth
with fistfuls of nuts from a plastic sack
of trail mix. Tomorrow he'll turn over
a year of his life that men never used
to dream of seeing. Tomorrow he won't
remember a thing. But right now he's lying
on the couch moaning with the pleasure
of still being so alive, his frayed blue robe
falling open to reveal a pair of pajamas
I know from my girlhood of riding his back
across the living room carpet while he growled
like a bear. Now his sock-mittened feet
twitch in ecstasy as he tells me about
the color of tonight's moon — *bitter orange,*
he says, *the sky like a pot of dark chocolate* —
hanging just outside the window.
Everyone in the house is busy making
their own sleeping sounds — the baby
like the faint wash of surf, my wife hopelessly
snoring away, my mother's CPAP machine
filling in the gaps with mechanized white noise
while my daughter rolls over to kick her
in the ribs — except this man, who's about
to crack open a carton of ice cream, who's
decided he'll sleep when he's dead.

Eating Sea Urchin

For the moment, speech is paused.
In the silence of the restaurant, we consider
the orange flesh, sagittal as a stilled
tongue, before placing it on our own.
Like most forms of magic, I've always believed
in words. For instance, the time you told me
it was over. Not that what you'd said
was true, but that by saying it everything instantly
was changed. To change where you are,
you might press your tongue's wet muscle
to a word round and glowing as the button
of an elevator and arrive a moment later
in a place unforeseen. Or use it to undo
your shirt one iridescent disc of a word
at a time until, tongue slipping delicately
in and out the stitching, you transform
into something that no longer has a skin.
But the tongue is not a blade: the blade
is the pain that opens the mouth and finds
the soft, forgiving muscle inside. *Uni,*
like any word resisted long enough, is salt
turned finally sweet on the tongue. It's alright
to say this is not the life you want for yourself
even one moment longer. This is how we each
might finally become different people—
with the gentle, wincing crack of a knife.

At Our Hotel Under the Volcano

We gather at the pool during the day,

and at night around the table   Adelina pulls
the lavender cigarillo from her pocket

like the scorpion that crept from my curtains

We're going to smoke this, she says   My friend
thought I shouldn't go to Mexico   Here, the man

in a wide hat is not just a man in a hat, but a man selling

bread from its brim   There was a time when I couldn't
recognize desire without madness, hunger

like bees swarming the guayaba outside

my window each morning   Here, everyone tells me
not to eat the food at the market   When Mateo

catches the scorpion in a yogurt cup

there is such tenderness in the way he observes
it lift its tiny tail   Here, the dogs are afraid

of the fireworks just like they are back home, curled

in balls beneath our chairs   The same tenderness
with which the cat very carefully places its delicate

claws on my thigh and sinks them in through my pants

Here, everyone tells me I have to try
the food at the market   My friend thought I might

cheat on my wife   Thought I might do something

stupid, crazy   What does it mean for the mountain
to smoke for years and never erupt?   Somehow, no matter

how much he eats, there is never a crumb

of pan dulce in Paco's mustache   Until tomorrow
morning when I wake with a fever and two red

lines running up my leg   Which could happen,

you know   Or Maribel laughing at me
as we eat our sopes, at the way I pause where her fingertips

have pressed the masa before I take my first bite

Playtime

Freezing my ass off in my daughter's tree house, the fat
mosquitoes moving so slowly I'm able to kill them

in the air, while my daughter's voice drifts to me
through the ferns and cedar boughs, the sound

of singing and imaginary chatter as she gathers
"berries" for us to "eat" and makes a "fire"

out of twigs. When she climbs the ladder back
into our lair, where my name is Violet and hers

is Jessie and both our parents are dead and no one
has been able to find Mother's will and Grandfather's

grand house burned down, she's holding a handful
of leaves. *This is all I could find for our dinner. I'm*

sorry, Violet. Spoken with a gravity so sincere
I am broken and offer my face to her, which she

knows means I'm asking for a kiss. And she gives it to me
before continuing her bustle, her unfolding of the picnic

cloth and fetching of the one tiny bowl. When she hands
me my portion of the leaves, they are crushed

and smell like every crushed leaf I've ever pressed
to my lips and not swallowed. We make chewing

sounds and toss the leaves behind us, letting them
fall to the ground as if we'd devoured them all.

Meat

a thistle : a burr : the fuzzed tines
of silver-tipped leaves : the soft-seeming
kind you might desire to rub your fingers
across in pleasure only to find
each tiny nerve stung with painful
shimmer : this is the feeling
that wakes me in the night : between
my legs : the folds inside the folds where
wetness hides its red head : no itch
to scratch : no rub that doesn't make me
burn more : my wife rolls over
as I creep from our bed : searching out
a bag of frozen peas : instead a round
of prosciutto delicately furred
with frost : still wrapped in butcher
paper by some man whose hands
sleep miles away : but first I crouch
to the bathroom floor : look with the half-
eye mirror of my shadow's
compact : there's nothing to finger beyond
the pink : tender : ageless : intricate : the more
I try to find the feeling the more diffuse
it becomes : interior or exterior : lateral or bi-
lateral : behind this door or that one : so back
to bed I go : put the meat between my legs : imagine
the pig : her long pale ears with their hidden
silk whorl : the rooting of her insistent
snout against my thigh : the old lady
whiskers that tremble and tangle as they
sprout overnight from her chinny-chin-chin

Summer, Again

I found the sunning snake like some trinket I'd lost

    and then forgotten: gilt earring, novelty

keychain, lover left in the sheets.

    It lay on the rock as if some lazy hand, lightest

of touch, had abandoned it there. The truth

    is that I haven't been inside my wife's body

in years. Imagine: living with a creek

    in your backyard—crush of wild mint

at the bank, slick stones pinned

    beneath its glossy lip, the ancient bugs

hatching from their own skins and dreaming

    the terror of fish, deep pools like dark yarn

gathered, the burble of it always in your ears—and you

    never dipping a finger inside. Instead, all summer,

every summer, another ending we didn't

ask for: the sickly-sweet thump of soft, feathered

bodies hitting the glass above our bed, the dry

heat rising from our stillness like dust.

Season Finale

We sit on the front stoop
and finish the bourbon.
The kids are inside watching
a nature show, the kind
where everything's already
dead: zoom-out to the coral reef
bleached, rainforest razed. Last night
on the sci-fi show we like to watch
together when the kids have fallen
asleep, the married couple lost
in space kissed after swimming
through an alien tar pit. I sat on the other
end of the couch from you
unable to imagine the tar pit
or the kissing, both as much a fantasy
as the murder show I turned on
when you went to bed. Of course, I don't want
to actually kill anything, but maybe
I do like imagining killing someone
as long as they're not really dead, as long as
they come back—*surprise!*—alive
in the first episode of the next season. But now,
through the open front door,
we can hear the nature narration, a tired
voice giving its grave warning and then
Borneo, like a safe word, but the opposite.
We've seen this episode, too, a million
times. It's the one where there's this bird
that clears a path before it does
its big mating dance. Borneo

doesn't have to mean the end
of the road. The end of roads. I say
that word I've always said to you,
since before we knew better.
It's not safe. There's nothing safe
about coming back from the brink.
But I do my little dance for you
on these cement steps—clink
jelly jars, give a wife's wink—resurrect
whatever tiny piece of this planet I can.

3,000 Miles Away from Home

I throw my leg over the bike's saddle
and, wheeling through the cold throb

of streetlights' shifting shadows
where kids in the park pump swings

in the dark, for one vainless moment
I am inside my body again, the neon

flutter-kicking its way on with a faint
tremble, like that day you stood

at our old apartment stove, topless
and frying eggs in a pair of boxer shorts,

your breasts just as beautiful and incongruous
as the smile you flash that gutters out

my heart these days, but back then breakfast
easily its own kind of drag show. I want

it back, that electric hum, my legs
pedaling faster than they ever have.

Diapause

My friend and I sit on the rocks across the river
from where a train overturned last spring, a
season in Montana when nothing's hatching
except the early stoneflies who descend to
the water with such spirited flesh that I long,
each year, to put a bug inside my mouth just
to taste something so furiously alive. Now it's
summer, and I'm here with my friend not so
much to swim as to praise what swimming
once felt like. We splash our feet in the shallows
and declare to each other the gratitude we feel
for every lover who ever hurt us—the drunk,
the dead, the simply but thoroughly cruel—
while boys almost too young to have really
hurt anyone launch their bodies through the
air and onto the current's waiting tongue.
There are those who won't speak to me now,
won't even whisper my name. But I say theirs.
And contained in each is a pleasure that would
be pain—the same persistent longing that
makes me want to trace the delicate vertebrae
descending below my friend's bikini clasp—
if I refused to allow myself to somehow love
them still. We agree: not everyone knows what
it is to be eaten alive by desire. But I hope they
sometimes think of my name, too, and, like
anything held too long in the mouth, it hurts.

Eating an Orange Before Getting
Out of the Swimming Pool

A sweetness so concentrated,
it's over almost before it's begun.
The heated accumulation
of fragrant peels on the wet
concrete's edge—like those months
we passed together—and the ants
that now pleasantly feast there.
Doesn't each brief pleasure deliver
us to the next? Lover, lover—
your wife and mine waiting
to meet us on the other side.

Googling My Ex

Not because I'm still in love with him, or
because I wish him ill. Not to smirk

by the insomniac's light, scrolling
through photos to learn if he's lost

all his hair or if his wife has managed
to pull a child from the flawless silk

top hat of her womb. I do it to see him
beyond that red truck he drove or the way

I thought I looked climbing into it, past
the stories of his dead father and the fantasies

I liked to make of holding that grown boy's
weeping face. I look now as I never could

back then when I, too, wished so badly for one
person in the world to see me for myself. I look

now to witness him living a life—a beautiful one—
we never could've imagined together.

Greek Chorus

Having not
touched myself
in some time
owing to
the erosion
of incremental
sadnesses
that can detach
a person
from their body
as cleanly
as a cliff
is sheared from
a coastline,
the doctor
informs me
that loving
myself
is now my
job. So I take up
my own two
fingers and
work them with
the seriousness
of earned salt
and an imaginary
salary
into the littoral
cavern of

my pussy. And
like a wave
that sweeps the
unsuspecting
from the rocky
breakwater,
quite suddenly
everyone
who has ever
fucked me is
fucking me
again—my
wife's warm breath
between my
thighs, crooning
softly I'm
a good girl
into the crook
of my lifted
knee, and each
lover who
came before
her, teasing
me open,
the little suck
and pop of it—
till I am
wide-eyed and
gulping.
Scholars say
in Homeric
tradition

when you recite
a character,
you not only
become that
character,
you join the
chorus of
any poet
that has sung
it before
you. Oh
rhapsode, trusted
storyteller,
traveling
staff in hand—
I take up
these voices
whispering,
crying,
laughing,
choking
on my pleasure.
I'm singing
the long
epic poem
of my body,
joining the
collective chorus,
becoming
the character
that once loved
me and now

remembers
how easy
it is—*good
girl*—to love
me still.

The Rats

They come home with our daughter
because there's no one at school
to feed them on the weekends.
They are mates, and like all true
companions they are devoted
and they bite. We set their cage
on the kitchen table and wait
for the weekend to end, for our girl
to fall asleep so we can talk
about god while the rats lick
the silver ball that delivers
the water one drop at a time.
There are so many points on which
you and I disagree: the value
of a clean counter, the purpose
of parent-teacher conferences,
what warrants a good cry or calling
you a name so cruel I make myself
whisper it through my teeth. God
is the least of it. When I think
I'm so angry I could hit you
in the face, you turn yours to me
with a look of disbelief. The rats,
meanwhile, have turned up the volume.
Tick, tick, says the silver ball
as their teeth click against it, thirsty
as ever, thirstier still at night
when the darkness wakes them.
And during the day, when they're curled
together in their flannel hammock,

head to tail, two furry apostrophes
possessing nothing but each other,
paws pressed together as if in prayer—
to what gods do they prostrate
themselves then? God of fidelity? God
of forgiveness? I lied when I said
I didn't believe. Who—even me,
the coldest of hearts—could turn away
from a sea parted, bread that multiplies
to answer need, water transformed
to the sweetest wine, the kind
that tastes better for each year
it's been left in the barrel?

Polished Rough

I know your childhood well enough—peaceful
two-story on a cul-de-sac—and can say
it's more than likely your mother never
took you along with her to the liquor store.
So you wouldn't have learned the almost-
pleasure of being pushed down the dim
aisle in a miniature cart, the heady smell
of cardboard boxes holding every drink
that hasn't yet been drunk, the wooden
counter and the man who used to reach
across its scuffed expanse to hand me
a candy: the flavor medicinal, the shape
and heft of pocket lozenges, the color like
a green beer bottle broken on the beach
and each piece polished rough by the ocean's
sand and stones. I've never seen them
anywhere else. But I remember the way I wanted
that hard little candy between my teeth,
not for what it was but for what it was
supposed to be: the promise of a sweetness
I knew it could never contain. And that's me.
That's my love. Not the kind you'd ever choose,
but one you've had to decide to want,
a piece of glass you wait so patiently to chew on.

Now that we've been married all these years,

tiny prop planes drag banners against
the sky selling us things we already have.

And whatever else crosses the landscape—
smoking engine of the trawler, polka-dotted

lantern fly, tendril of melted ice cream
snail-stickying your wrist's golden

expanse—is just one more thing I don't have
a choice about loving. I know there was a time

before I met you, but that fact is like knowing
that the length of my veins could wrap around

the Earth four times or that each year on Saturn
it rains ten million tons of diamonds—imaginable,

but just barely. Because love before your arrival
had been an idiopathic thing, pain without

a diagnosable source, a sensation that divided me
from the people I loved because I was the only one

who could feel it. When some people get married,
they're making a pact with another person.

When I married you, I made a pact with the world.
I live in it now, and refuse myself nothing.

Notes

The title of the poem *"Lonely women make good lovers,"* comes from the song of the same name, written by Freddy Weller and Spooner Oldham. It was first recorded by Bob Luman and later covered by Steve Wariner. I believe I've heard both versions play on my beloved, old school Western Montana country music station, The Ranch 107.1.

"Spa Days" and its sense of self-discovery is indebted to Mark Spero and to a risky and wonderful poem of his own that he brought into our workshop while I was a Visiting Professor at the University of Montana.

The title of the poem "Sehnsucht" is a German word that has no direct translation into English but can be described as an unsatisfiable longing.

"Love Letter to a Friend I Cannot Reach" is for Kiran Rikhye.

"Brace Cove" was written after the painting "Brace's Rock" by Fitz Henry Lane, which I viewed at the Cape Ann Museum in Gloucester, MA, while on a residency at the T.S. Eliot House in October of 2023.

"The day after your mom dies, I go to see the witches," is for Ashley Sherburne and in memory of her mother, April Leach.

It was a privilege to publicly work through the blind spots and missteps (many remain, I'm sure) of "Boat Puller / Bird Woman / Madame Charbonneau" through *Midst*'s interactive timelapse software. Annelyse Gelman has done the poetry

75

community a service by providing this platform for witnessing the creation and revision of poems in real time. You can visit www.midst.press to see how I wrote this poem from, as they say, "start to finish, blank page to final draft, and every edit in between." The texts quoted in this poem come from the following sources: the journals of William Clark, recorded during the Lewis and Clark expedition; a since-edited version of the Wikipedia entry for the Sacagawea dollar; a 2010 *Coin World* article by Steve Roach on coin design themes; a 2015 *Washington Post* article by Dan Murano on the photographer Edward Curtis; and the journals of Meriwether Lewis, recorded during the Lewis and Clark expedition.

"Walking Lessons" was written with gratitude for the enduring forgiveness and friendship of H.R.

"Pregnant Girl Creek" is in memory of Julie Ann Shaffer. Always.

"Diapause" is for Henrietta Goodman.

"Greek Chorus" is indebted to David Naimon and Alice Oswald, whose conversation on the podcast *Between the Covers* inspired the rhetorical framework that allowed this poem to find its voice(s).

Acknowledgments

Grateful acknowledgment is made to the editors of the following publications, in which these works or earlier versions of them previously appeared:

32 Poems: "Cremello Horse";
The Adroit Journal: "Pregnant Girl Creek";
Alaska Quarterly Review: "Diapause";
American Chordata: "*Lonely women make good lovers,*";
The Amsterdam Review: "Sehnsucht";
Bennington Review: "Polished Rough";
BOAAT: "The Magician at the Woodpile";
The Cincinnati Review: "Eating Sea Urchin," "Greek Chorus," "Poikilothermic";
Copper Nickel: "Meat";
The Cortland Review: "Walking Lessons";
Four Way Review: "In the Outdoor Shower with My Pregnant Wife," "With Garbo in Palm Springs";
Gulf Coast: "Interview";
High Country News: "At My Daughter's Riding Lesson";
Interim: "Season Finale";
The Massachusetts Review: "I, too, took pictures of my body";
Midst: "Boat Puller / Bird Woman / Madame Charbonneau";
On the Seawall: "Live Webcam: Ponte Delle Guglie, Venice, March 2020";
Orion Magazine: "At Forty, the Mountains Are More Green";
Pleiades: "Brace Cove," "Summer, Again";
Poet Lore: "At Our Hotel Under the Volcano," "Multi-Generational Household";
Poetry: "Selfishness";
Prairie Schooner: "Googling My Ex";

Rhino: "The Wound";
River Mouth Review: "Love Letter to a Friend I Cannot Reach";
Salamander: "Bleeding";
Southern Indiana Review: "3,000 Miles Away from Home," "I
    wasn't trying to steal her boyfriend,";
The Common: "Washing My Daughter's Laundry," "I didn't
    know what I didn't know," "Spa Days";
The Seventh Wave: "My Mother Bought Me a Scarf";
The Yale Review: "Getting Back Together";
Virginia Quarterly Review: "Crossing";
Water~Stone Review: "Playtime";
Zócalo Public Square: "I Let Her Let Them."

"Emesis" and "The Rats" were each featured as part of the Academy of American Poets' *Poem-A-Day* series.

"At Forty, the Mountains Are More Green" was featured on the podcast *The Slowdown*.

I am grateful to the following institutions, which provided vital fellowships, residencies, and financial support that nurtured the writing of this book: the Virginia Center for the Creative Arts, the SWWIM residency at The Betsy-South Beach, the T.S. Eliot House, the Storyknife Writers Retreat, and the Montana Arts Council.

I can definitively say that many of these poems would not exist, and certainly would not be their best selves, without the counsel and constant inspiration provided by my Poetry Gals: Gabrielle Bates, Rachel Edelman, and Abi Pollokoff. I would be lost without you.

There are many editors and friends—too many to thank here—

who read these poems and offered encouragement, advice, and fellowship. Erika Meitner, you've been here for the long haul, and my gratitude for you is real. Esther Lin, you pushed me and this book over the finish line just when I needed a shove.

My *Poetry Northwest* team is the bedrock of my literary community, and I am grateful to my staff for always challenging me, keeping me on my toes, catching my mistakes, and, most importantly, being beside me in the fight. There are no poems without community, and you all are mine.

To my students, near and far: During the writing of this book, the example of your work urged me to take risks, embrace forgotten wildnesses, and to stay humble and vulnerable on the page. I am amazed by your talent and fearlessness.

Elizabeth Urschel, you are the best therapist in the world. Our conversations have given me the permission not only to feel, but also to write into the many questions that deep feeling lays bare. Thank you—these poems are better, and I am better, because of you.

Many of these poems address old friends and old friendships, some of which I've screwed up more than once. Your forgiveness—and the forgiveness bestowed by time—is something I cherish.

My parents helped my family survive tremendous challenges during the years I was writing these poems. And my children brought joy even in moments of nearly unbearable heartache. I am so grateful for our messy, multi-generational life together.

Sarah, you are the only one for me. I knew it then, and I know it more every day. This book is for you.

About the Author

Keetje Kuipers is the author of three previous books of poems, all from BOA Editions. The recipient of a Pushcart Prize, her poems, essays, and stories have appeared in such publications as *Poetry*, *Virginia Quarterly Review*, *The Yale Review*, *The New York Times Magazine*, and *Best American Poetry*. Keetje previously served on the board of the National Book Critics Circle and has been the recipient of a Wallace Stegner Fellowship, a National Endowment for the Arts Literature Fellowship, and the Margery Davis Boyden Wilderness Writing Residency. Currently the editor of *Poetry Northwest*, Keetje teaches at universities and conferences around the world, including at the dual-language writers' gathering Under the Volcano in Tepoztlán, Mexico. Her home is in Missoula, Montana, on the land of the Salish and Kalispel peoples and directly at the foot of the Rattlesnake Wilderness. She lives there with her wife and their two children, where she co-directs the Headwaters Reading Series for Health and Well-Being and keeps an eye out for bears in her backyard.

BOA Editions, Ltd. American Poets
Continuum Series

No. 1 *The Fuhrer Bunker: A Cycle of Poems in Progress*
W. D. Snodgrass

No. 2 *She*
M. L. Rosenthal

No. 3 *Living With Distance*
Ralph J. Mills, Jr.

No. 4 *Not Just Any Death*
Michael Waters

No. 5 *That Was Then: New and Selected Poems*
Isabella Gardner

No. 6 *Things That Happen Where There Aren't Any People*
William Stafford

No. 7 *The Bridge of Change: Poems 1974–1980*
John Logan

No. 8 *Signatures*
Joseph Stroud

No. 9 *People Live Here: Selected Poems 1949–1983*
Louis Simpson

No. 10 *Yin*
Carolyn Kizer

No. 11 *Duhamel: Ideas of Order in Little Canada*
Bill Tremblay

No. 12 *Seeing It Was So*
Anthony Piccione

No. 13 *Hyam Plutzik: The Collected Poems*

No. 14 *Good Woman: Poems and a Memoir 1969–1980*
Lucille Clifton

No. 15 *Next: New Poems*
Lucille Clifton

No. 16 *Roxa: Voices of the Culver Family*
William B. Patrick

No. 17 *John Logan: The Collected Poems*

No. 18 Isabella Gardner: The Collected Poems

No. 19 *The Sunken Lightship*
Peter Makuck

No. 20 *The City in Which I Love You*
Li-Young Lee

No. 21 *Quilting: Poems 1987–1990*
Lucille Clifton

No. 22 *John Logan: The Collected Fiction*

No. 23 *Shenandoah and Other Verse Plays*
Delmore Schwartz

No. 24 *Nobody Lives on Arthur Godfrey Boulevard*
Gerald Costanzo

No. 25 *The Book of Names: New and Selected Poems*
Barton Sutter

No. 26 *Each in His Season*
W. D. Snodgrass

No. 27 *Wordworks: Poems Selected and New*
Richard Kostelanetz

No. 28 *What We Carry*
Dorianne Laux

No. 29 *Red Suitcase*
Naomi Shihab Nye

No. 30 *Song*
Brigit Pegeen Kelly

No. 31 *The Fuehrer Bunker: The Complete Cycle*
W. D. Snodgrass

No. 32 *For the Kingdom*
Anthony Piccione

No. 33 *The Quicken Tree*
Bill Knott

No. 34 *These Upraised Hands*
William B. Patrick

No. 35 *Crazy Horse in Stillness*
William Heyen

No. 36 *Quick, Now, Always*
Mark Irwin

No. 37 *I Have Tasted the Apple*
Mary Crow

No. 38 *The Terrible Stories*
Lucille Clifton

No. 39 *The Heat of Arrivals*
Ray Gonzalez

No. 40 *Jimmy & Rita*
Kim Addonizio

No. 41 *Green Ash, Red Maple, Black Gum*
Michael Waters

No. 42 *Against Distance*
Peter Makuck

No. 43 *The Night Path*
Laurie Kutchins

No. 44 *Radiography*
Bruce Bond

No. 45 *At My Ease: Uncollected Poems of the Fifties and Sixties*
David Ignatow

No. 46 *Trillium*
Richard Foerster

No. 47 *Fuel*
Naomi Shihab Nye

No. 48 *Gratitude*
Sam Hamill

No. 49 *Diana, Charles, & the Queen*
William Heyen

No. 50 *Plus Shipping*
Bob Hicok

No. 51 *Cabato Sentora*
Ray Gonzalez

No. 52 *We Didn't Come Here for This*
William B. Patrick

No. 53 *The Vandals*
Alan Michael Parker

No. 54 *To Get Here*
Wendy Mnookin

No. 55 *Living Is What I Wanted:
Last Poems*
David Ignatow

No. 56 *Dusty Angel*
Michael Blumenthal

No. 57 *The Tiger Iris*
Joan Swift

No. 58 *White City*
Mark Irwin

No. 59 *Laugh at the End of the
World: Collected Comic
Poems 1969–1999*
Bill Knott

No. 60 *Blessing the Boats: New
and Selected Poems:
1988–2000*
Lucille Clifton

No. 61 *Tell Me*
Kim Addonizio

No. 62 *Smoke*
Dorianne Laux

No. 63 *Parthenopi: New and
Selected Poems*
Michael Waters

No. 64 *Rancho Notorious*
Richard Garcia

No. 65 *Jam*
Joe-Anne McLaughlin

No. 66 *A. Poulin, Jr. Selected
Poems*
Edited, with an
Introduction by
Michael Waters

No. 67 *Small Gods of Grief*
Laure-Anne Bosselaar

No. 68 *Book of My Nights*
Li-Young Lee

No. 69 *Tulip Farms and Leper
Colonies*
Charles Harper Webb

No. 70 *Double Going*
Richard Foerster

No. 71 *What He Took*
Wendy Mnookin

No. 72 *The Hawk Temple at
Tierra Grande*
Ray Gonzalez

No. 73 *Mules of Love*
Ellen Bass

No. 74 *The Guests at the Gate*
Anthony Piccione

No. 75 *Dumb Luck*
Sam Hamill

No. 76 *Love Song with Motor
Vehicles*
Alan Michael Parker

No. 77 *Life Watch*
Willis Barnstone

No. 78 *The Owner of the House:
New Collected Poems
1940–2001*
Louis Simpson

No. 79 *Is*
Wayne Dodd

No. 80 *Late*
Cecilia Woloch

No. 81 *Precipitates*
Debra Kang Dean

No. 82 *The Orchard*
Brigit Pegeen Kelly

No. 83 *Bright Hunger*
Mark Irwin

No. 84 *Desire Lines: New and
Selected Poems*
Lola Haskins

No. 85 *Curious Conduct*
Jeanne Marie Beaumont

No. 86 *Mercy*
Lucille Clifton

No. 87 *Model Homes*
Wayne Koestenbaum

No. 88 *Farewell to the Starlight
in Whiskey*
Barton Sutter

No. 89 *Angels for the Burning*
David Mura

No. 90 *The Rooster's Wife*
Russell Edson

No. 91 *American Children*
Jim Simmerman

No. 92 *Postcards from the
Interior*
Wyn Cooper

No. 93 *You & Yours*
Naomi Shihab Nye

No. 94 *Consideration of the
Guitar: New and Selected
Poems 1986–2005*
Ray Gonzalez

No. 95 *Off-Season in the
Promised Land*
Peter Makuck

No. 96 *The Hoopoe's Crown*
Jacqueline Osherow

No. 97 *Not for Specialists:
New and Selected Poems*
W. D. Snodgrass

No. 98 *Splendor*
Steve Kronen

No. 99 *Woman Crossing a Field*
Deena Linett

No. 100 *The Burning of Troy*
Richard Foerster

No. 101 *Darling Vulgarity*
Michael Waters

No. 102 *The Persistence of Objects*
Richard Garcia

No. 103 *Slope of the Child
Everlasting*
Laurie Kutchins

No. 104 *Broken Hallelujahs*
Sean Thomas
Dougherty

No. 105 *Peeping Tom's Cabin:
Comic Verse 1928–2008*
X. J. Kennedy

No. 106 *Disclamor*
G.C. Waldrep

No. 107 *Encouragement for a Man Falling to His Death*
Christopher Kennedy

No. 108 *Sleeping with Houdini*
Nin Andrews

No. 109 *Nomina*
Karen Volkman

No. 110 *The Fortieth Day*
Kazim Ali

No. 111 *Elephants & Butterflies*
Alan Michael Parker

No. 112 *Voices*
Lucille Clifton

No. 113 *The Moon Makes Its Own Plea*
Wendy Mnookin

No. 114 *The Heaven-Sent Leaf*
Katy Lederer

No. 115 *Struggling Times*
Louis Simpson

No. 116 *And*
Michael Blumenthal

No. 117 *Carpathia*
Cecilia Woloch

No. 118 *Seasons of Lotus, Seasons of Bone*
Matthew Shenoda

No. 119 *Sharp Stars*
Sharon Bryan

No. 120 *Cool Auditor*
Ray Gonzalez

No. 121 *Long Lens: New and Selected Poems*
Peter Makuck

No. 122 *Chaos Is the New Calm*
Wyn Cooper

No. 123 *Diwata*
Barbara Jane Reyes

No. 124 *Burning of the Three Fires*
Jeanne Marie Beaumont

No. 125 *Sasha Sings the Laundry on the Line*
Sean Thomas Dougherty

No. 126 *Your Father on the Train of Ghosts*
G.C. Waldrep and John Gallaher

No. 127 *Ennui Prophet*
Christopher Kennedy

No. 128 *Transfer*
Naomi Shihab Nye

No. 129 *Gospel Night*
Michael Waters

No. 130 *The Hands of Strangers: Poems from the Nursing Home*
Janice N. Harrington

No. 131 *Kingdom Animalia*
Aracelis Girmay

No. 132 *True Faith*
Ira Sadoff

No. 133 *The Reindeer Camps and Other Poems*
Barton Sutter

No. 134 *The Collected Poems of Lucille Clifton: 1965–2010*

No. 135 *To Keep Love Blurry*
Craig Morgan Teicher

No. 136 *Theophobia*
Bruce Beasley

No. 137 *Refuge*
Adrie Kusserow

No. 138 *The Book of Goodbyes*
Jillian Weise

No. 139 *Birth Marks*
Jim Daniels

No. 140 *No Need of Sympathy*
Fleda Brown

No. 141 *There's a Box in the Garage You Can Beat with a Stick*
Michael Teig

No. 142 *The Keys to the Jail*
Keetje Kuipers

No. 143 *All You Ask for Is Longing: New and Selected Poems 1994–2014*
Sean Thomas Dougherty

No. 144 *Copia*
Erika Meitner

No. 145 *The Chair: Prose Poems*
Richard Garcia

No. 146 *In a Landscape*
John Gallaher

No. 147 *Fanny Says*
Nickole Brown

No. 148 *Why God Is a Woman*
Nin Andrews

No. 149 *Testament*
G.C. Waldrep

No. 150 *I'm No Longer Troubled by the Extravagance*
Rick Bursky

No. 151 *Antidote for Night*
Marsha de la O

No. 152 *Beautiful Wall*
Ray Gonzalez

No. 153 *the black maria*
Aracelis Girmay

No. 154 *Celestial Joyride*
Michael Waters

No. 155 *Whereso*
Karen Volkman

No. 156 *The Day's Last Light Reddens the Leaves of the Copper Beech*
Stephen Dobyns

No. 157 *The End of Pink*
Kathryn Nuernberger

No. 158 *Mandatory Evacuation*
Peter Makuck

No. 159 *Primitive: The Art and Life of Horace H. Pippin*
Janice N. Harrington

No. 160 *The Trembling Answers*
Craig Morgan Teicher

No. 161 *Bye-Bye Land*
Christian Barter

No. 162 *Sky Country*
Christine Kitano

No. 163 *All Soul Parts Returned*
Bruce Beasley

No. 164 *The Smoke of Horses*
Charles Rafferty

No. 165 *The Second O of Sorrow*
Sean Thomas
Dougherty

No. 166 *Holy Moly Carry Me*
Erika Meitner

No. 167 *Clues from the Animal
Kingdom*
Christopher Kennedy

No. 168 *Dresses from the Old
Country*
Laura Read

No. 169 *In Country*
Hugh Martin

No. 170 *The Tiny Journalist*
Naomi Shihab Nye

No. 171 *All Its Charms*
Keetje Kuipers

No. 172 *Night Angler*
Geffrey Davis

No. 173 *The Human Half*
Deborah Brown

No. 174 *Cyborg Detective*
Jillian Weise

No. 175 *On the Shores of Welcome
Home*
Bruce Weigl

No. 176 *Rue*
Kathryn Nuernberger

No. 177 *Let's Become a Ghost
Story*
Rick Bursky

No. 178 *Year of the Dog*
Deborah Paredez

No. 179 *Brand New Spacesuit*
John Gallaher

No. 180 *How to Carry Water:
Selected Poems of Lucille
Clifton*
Edited, with an
Introduction by
Aracelis Girmay

No. 181 *Caw*
Michael Waters

No. 182 *Letters to a Young Brown
Girl*
Barbara Jane Reyes

No. 183 *Mother Country*
Elana Bell

No. 184 *Welcome to Sonnetville,
New Jersey*
Craig Morgan Teicher

No. 185 *I Am Not Trying to Hide
My
Hungers from the World*
Kendra DeColo

No. 186 *The Naomi Letters*
Rachel Mennies

No. 187 *Tenderness*
Derrick Austin

No. 188 *Ceive*
B.K. Fischer

No. 189 *Diamonds*
Camille Guthrie

No. 190 *A Cluster of Noisy Planets*
Charles Rafferty

No. 191 *Useful Junk*
Erika Meitner

No. 192 *Field Notes from the Flood Zone*
Heather Sellers

No. 193 *A Season in Hell with Rimbaud*
Dustin Pearson

No. 194 *Your Emergency Contact Has Experienced an Emergency*
Chen Chen

No. 195 *A Tinderbox in Three Acts*
Cynthia Dewi Oka

No. 196 *Little Mr. Prose Poem: Selected Poems of Russell Edson*
Edited by Craig Morgan Teicher

No. 197 *The Dug-Up Gun Museum*
Matt Donovan

No. 198 *Four in Hand*
Alicia Mountain

No. 199 *Buffalo Girl*
Jessica Q. Stark

No. 200 *Nomenclatures of Invisibility*
Mahtem Shiferraw

No. 201 *Flare, Corona*
Jeannine Hall Gailey

No. 202 *Death Prefers the Minor Keys*
Sean Thomas Dougherty

No. 203 *Desire Museum*
Danielle Deulen

No. 204 *Transitory*
Subhaga Crystal Bacon

No. 205 *Every Hard Sweetness*
Sheila Carter-Jones

No. 206 *Blue on a Blue Palette*
Lynne Thompson

No. 207 *One Wild Word Away*
Geffrey Davis

No. 208 *The Strange God Who Makes Us*
Christopher Kennedy

No. 209 *Our Splendid Failure to Do the Impossible*
Rebecca Lindenberg

No. 210 *Yard Show*
Janice N. Harrington

No. 211 *The Last Song of the World*
Joseph Fasano

No. 212 *Lonely Women Make Good Lovers*
Keetje Kuipers

Colophon

BOA Editions, Ltd., a not-for-profit publisher of poetry and other literary works, fosters readership and appreciation of contemporary literature. By identifying, cultivating, and publishing both new and established poets and selecting authors of unique literary talent, BOA brings high-quality literature to the public.

Support for this effort comes from the sale of its publications, grant funding, and private donations.

The publication of this book is made possible, in part, by the special support of the following individuals:

Anonymous

Angela Bonazinga & Catherine Lewis

Ralph Black & Susan Murphy

Chris Dahl, *in honor of Chuck Hertrick*

Jonathan Everitt

David Fraher, *in memory of A. Poulin Jr.*

Bonnie Garner

Jenny Graber

James Hale

Peg Heminway

Nora A. Jones

Joe & Dale Klein

Barbara Lovenheim, *in memory of John Lovenheim*

Joe McElveney

Daniel M. Meyers, *in honor of J. Shepard Skiff*

Boo Poulin, *in memory of A. Poulin Jr.*

Deborah Ronnen

John H. Schultz

Robert Thomas

Lynne Thompson

William Waddell & Linda Rubel

Michael Waters & Mihaela Moscaliuc

www.ingramcontent.com/pod-product-compliance
Lightning Source LLC
Jackson TN
JSHW080758130525
84337JS00002B/21